to _____

from _____

Published by Sourcebooks, Inc.
P.O. Box 4410, Naperville, Illinois 60567–4410
(630) 961–3900
Fax: (630) 961–2168
www.sourcebooks.com

ISBN-13: 978-1-4022-0738-9
ISBN-10: 1-4022-0738-7

Printed and bound in China
LP 10 9 8 7 6 5 4 3 2 1

You're My Friend

Be Paws

by Jeannie Schick-Jacobowitz and
Susie Schick-Pierce

illustrations by Robin Bielefeld

SOURCEBOOKS, INC.®
NAPERVILLE, ILLINOIS

You're My Friend

Be Paws

You know
what's
important
in life

You're My Friend

Be Paws

You always
listen to my
fireside
chats

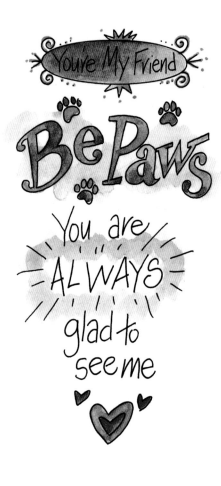

You never
say
diet!

You're My Friend

Be Paws

You know how
to dance through
the puddles
in life

You're My Friend

Be Paws

You're
my most
devoted
friend

You're My Friend

Be Paws

Your
playfulness
is
contagious

You accept
me as I am...
wrinkles
and all

You're My Friend

Be Paws

You
make
my day

You're My Friend

BePaws

You can
make me
howl

You're My Friend

Be Paws

You deserve
to be
spoiled

You're My Friend

Be Paws

You
can always
read my
moods

You're My Friend

Be Paws

You show
me that love
comes in all
shapes and
sizes

You're My Friend

Be Paws

Life is
more fun
with you by
my side

You're My Friend

Be Paws

You
always
stand by
me

You're My Friend

Be Paws

You know that a faithful friend is the best medicine

You're My Friend

BePaws

You're all
ears when
I need a
good listener

blah... blah.. blah..

You're My Friend

Be Paws

You show
me
the value
of patience

You're My Friend

Be Paws

You
follow
your bliss

You're My Friend

Be Paws

Life with
you is an

Adventure!

You're My Friend

BePaws

To me you're
the
Best in Show,

Best in Breed,
Best in World!

Jeannie Schick-Jacobowitz and Susie Schick-Pierce are sisters, collaborators, and a powerful creative team. They have worked together on numerous bestselling gift books and mini-books.

Robin Bielefeld has a degree in Commercial Art, and has worked in advertising, and as a freelance illustrator.